TESTIMONY OF A DIVORCEE

TESTIMONY OF A DIVORCEE

The Source of Happiness Lies Within Oneself

Rendani Ratshibvumo

EXCELLER BOOKS®
A GLOBAL PRESS

Testimony of a Divorcee

The Source of Happiness Lies Within Oneself

Cover by Exceller Books using resources from Pixabay.com

ISBN: 978-81-19524-47-1

First published in India in 2025 by Exceller Books,
An imprint of GE Group

Address: G1, Dream Apartment, Degree College Road, Belgharia,
Kolkata, 700056, India
www.excellerbooks.com

EXCELLER BOOKS®
A GLOBAL PRESS

Dedication

This book is dedicated to all those who are wounded and broken, seeking to be better and do better.

Acknowledgement

I want to thank:

- My partner, Mpho, for reading everything I write, even when she doesn't feel like it.
- My parents for always inspiring me in their own unique ways.
- My sisters, Nale, Rabe, and Fhulu, for believing in my desired realities without any doubts.
- My best friends, Rofhiwa, Nareen, and Hunadi.
- My acquired family, Ayasha, Amaarah, and Amaad.
- All of my ex-girlfriends and one-nightstands—you each contributed immensely to my journey of self-discovery.

I want to express my deepest gratitude to God, as He created me whole.

Why this book?

'Testimony of a Divorcee' was not something I had planned or foreseen coming into my life; when I did get married, the perceived outcome was not ending up in divorce. My marriage was very brief. I was married on the 29th of March 2019 in the beautiful city of Cape Town. Flying with my whole family to Cape Town from Ha-Mphego Thohoyandou was the most remarkable experience.

My married life was instead a period of awakening. I was sleeping without awareness of my slumber. The revelation to share my experiences and my journey was in the pursuit of helping seekers who might be in the same circumstances that I was in; they can use this as a reference or a learning guide to ease their way into finding themselves.

This book will not provide all the answers, but I pray that the universe opens some pathways and that some secrets will be revealed to you as you read this book.

This is my truth.

Contents

1| Meet My Family

I am Rendani Ratshibvumo, born in a small village in Thohoyandou town (Ha-Mphego) in Limpopo Province, South Africa. I had what I considered an abnormal upbringing; everything in my family seemed quite different from those around me. I was raised by what felt like a single parent to a 3-year-old girl, and I am sure you are puzzled why I would phrase it in that manner; let me explain a bit of that.

I am a first-born child to my parents, a second-born child to my mother, and a third-born child to my father. You can imagine the dynamics and questions that could arise from the fragile mind of a three-year-old faced with that family tree. My mother primarily raised me, but my father was always there in the background, and my sisters and I would see him a couple of times a year.

We did not stay with my father until I was around 14. We had quite an estranged relationship for most of my life. Even as I author this book at 33, our relationship is still at the take-off level. I still have loads of healing to do. I might be running out of time, as he is already 64. My guardian angels, please step on the accelerator in this aspect of my life because it will be harder to improve this relationship once he is no longer on this earth.

Time is one of those resources that most of us take for granted in so many ways; each day, we lose hours doing things that do not progress our purpose, and we have normalised it; we do it without shame or guilt. So, the universe, please grant me the spirit of urgency so I may go at your pace and not my own. Amen.

My mother provided everything for my three sisters and me. She did the best she could with the resources she could access, and I thank God for her each day. She was a domestic worker raising four daughters on her own. We did not go a day without food, nor did we ever have clothes on our backs or shelter; she provided our basic needs. My father always bought clothes for us at the end of the year for Christmas; he always brought the trendiest fashion items each year. He did not compromise on that, and he did not mind doing the shopping for us.

I spent most afternoons of my childhood with my grandmother (God bless her soul); my mother had to work, my sister went to school, and my grandmother took care of me until either my mother or my sister came to fetch me.

I have always been empathic, shy, and soft-spoken. I had a challenging time relating to other children. Do not get me wrong; I was highly active with the neighbours of my age group during playtime. But I could not shake up the emptiness; I always felt like an outcast. It was always as if I never belonged anywhere. No matter how hard I tried, that emptiness inside me remained.

My mother is a caring, nurturing, and God-fearing woman; she provided a warm home for us, even when days were dark, she always showed up when it came to her girls, and we were always her motivation; we still. She always drew her strength from God through prayer and fasting, and I learned about her secret weapon as I grew older.

I had a close relationship with her; she would share her pains, concerns, and happiness with my sisters and me. I could sense each time she was not happy; I am still able to do that.

My father worked away from home when he would get some time off and come to visit us, but he stayed with his parents in the house that my mother and sisters eventually moved into.

Every time he visited us, I would hide away. He would try to reach out to me, and he would only win if he gave me money. I would go and sit with him, and then I would have a problem when he had to leave. I spent half his visiting time hiding away, and by the time I had warmed up to him, it was time to go. My relationship with my father was touch and go for most of my childhood.

I had a close relationship with my mother, but because she was firm or I did not want to burden her with my issues while knowing what trouble came with raising us, I hardly spoke my mind. I was always what was considered an obedient child. I did as I was told; I followed her rules most of my life. I became a little miss independent.

As I grew older, it took away my ability to be vulnerable. I have always been independent, did things on my own, and hardly asked for help. I always figured things out on my own. Even at this age, I am still struggling to overcome being vulnerable. This has negatively affected my relationships as an adult; I was always the one who had her shit together even though I would be falling apart on the inside.

There is a ten-year age gap between my elder sister and me; she left for university when I was seven and had two younger siblings, strengthening my need to be independent.

At the age of ten, I remember asking my mother to teach me basic cooking skills; that way, I could be more helpful in the house; she did not have to come home from a long day of cleaning, washing, and cooking for another family and do more cooking at home. And she did just that, and I helped her cook a couple of days a week. As a result, I developed a love for cooking; those who have spent time with me will confess that I am a feeder. I express my love by preparing meals and making sure people are fed.

My mother is still the best cook I know, and she will feed the heaven out of you. To this day, every time my sisters and I go to my mother's house, we place our orders before we get there so that by our time of arrival, everything is ready for us to feast on. Visiting her for a weekend will result in weight gain because you will be eating all the time.

I am currently a dietitian by profession, and every nutrition knowledge and wisdom I have accumulated in my practice goes outside the window whenever I am at home. Her secret ingredient when cooking meat of any kind is fat. She makes the fat taste so good; even today, she does not allow me to clean the tripe because I would remove all the visible fat, and she said I removed all the goodness from the meat. I did not like vegetables as a child. I would sleep hungry if we were eating them for dinner. I only appreciated them as I got older, and her vegetables are the best; she has no recipes, no Google; she cooks out of intuition, which is just God-given wisdom.

As I grew older, I only got closer to my sister; I respected her much, like my mother. As we grew more intimate in my high school years, I would babysit her son during school holidays, but still, I could not share my deepest thoughts and feelings with her. When I think about it now, it was such a shame. I think she would have gained as much insight from me as I did from her.

My sister and I have much in common, especially our personality traits. We are extremely ambitious and have a tough time expressing ourselves. We treat our mother like the Goddess; she is the centre of our universe. We worked hard to make her life easier, from school to the workplace. Our goal was to make sure that our mother did not have to work in her life. She worked hard before we were born, and we wanted to take care of her.

I have always enjoyed my younger sisters' relationship with our mother. They shared everything with her, and they still do. They would even share my secrets with her, which I could never do. Our personalities are so different; they are outgoing, and I am reserved. Everything that I did not do growing up, they are doing, I mean, they challenged my mother and most of the time got away with it; I mean, Mom, you would not let me get away with that, but then again, I never challenged her decisions as they do. They grew up to be such amazing young women of which we are proud.

As I walk down memory lane, I find out that my relationship issues run deep. I was so much in my head that my relationship with my grandparents seemed like a blur. I know my maternal grandmother took care of me as a child, but even though I have no memory of it, I need hypnosis to find out what is hidden deep in my subconscious and why is it hidden there in the first place. I might be going for therapy after authoring this book. I will surely keep you updated on what I find out.

I became closer to my maternal grandfather towards his last days. I tried to visit him whenever I went back to my home village, mainly because my mother would tell him about my return. If I did not see him, he would complain to my mother. My mother would not have told him about my return to avoid confrontation if I had not visited him.

After his passing, we became even closer. In African culture, your body dies, but your spirit continues to live (ancestors). I was so fortunate to meet with him from a spiritual realm that I did not take into grasp until recent years. Thank you, Gugu (grandparent in Tshivenda), for opening that pathway for me.

From my paternal side, things were rocky from the start. As the first child born after my father's divorce, I felt as if my grandmother was never going to accept me. I reminded her of why things ended between my father and his first wife. Things got worse when we had to move in with my father and his parents. My father is the youngest son, and in Tshivenda tradition, he is responsible for taking care of his parents.

To this day, I do not think my parents ever planned for us to move into my father's home; the universe made that happen. In the year 2000, South Africa experienced heavy rains resulting in devastating flooding in the history of our country; hundreds of people lost their lives. Others were fortunate to lose only their properties; my family was part of the lucky group who lost their home. I say that I am blessed because we survived; I can share my story through the grace of life that I still have. Thank you, God, for preserving my family.

Together with our mother, my siblings and I had to move back to my maternal grandparents' home. I stayed there for two years. Life was not as I had known it. I was used to a small family of four. Now, we are a family of ten people. Tension was inevitable, and it did arise. Rebuilding our home would be too expensive, and my father's house was our best option.

Now, living with my paternal grandparents posed whole new challenges. My grandmother had not accepted my mother, which made it difficult for me to be closer to her as I was overprotective of my mother. My grandmother and I were civil toward each other but never had a relationship. My grandfather, on the other hand, was a loner. He woke up every morning in his active days and went out with the cattle; he was a shepherd; he would come home to eat and sleep. He would only speak if my grandmother had prepared a vegetable dish for him; he hated vegetables and wanted to eat meat daily but never financially contributed to the house. That was also a lost opportunity for me; they are all gone, and I cannot do anything about it. I do not want the same to happen between my father and me.

My family has always been divided, from aunties to uncles. As far as I can remember, there has always been tension; as grandchildren of my maternal grandfather, we vowed to be different from our parents after our grandfather's passing and stick together even if our parents were apart. We started a foundation (NTHAMBELENI FOUNDATION) in honour of his memory; the aim was to assist one another socially and financially; by the grace of God given to our grandfather's spirit, the foundation is still active, even though membership is not as when we started but those who are still in it are fighting for our grandfather's memory, all he ever wanted was for his children and their families to be together.

I have the worst social skills; making friends is a trial. However, I am improving at initiating conversations; I believe my field of work has opened me up a little, not forgetting a drink or two here and there. I have always been a shy child; I would hide away every time a guest walked into our home; one of my mother's household rules was that we all must greet the guests individually. I would keep busy until she called me out by name to welcome the guest; it was not a lack of manners but confidence, I suppose.

From primary to high school, making friends was difficult for me. Things got better in university primarily because you could not shut me up after a drink or two. I became aware of what alcohol did to my confidence, which led to me drinking more often. Drinking led to parties and some form of friendships here and there. But the companies always involved drinking, which became my norm for over five years. I still struggle with staying connected with people, especially if they are physically distant, even with technological advancement.

2| Unlucky in Love

I have always been a late bloomer; I started dating in high school at fifteen, in tenth grade. All my friends had started dating; I was just not interested. When I started dating, things did not work out well for me for at least three years. After two months of dating, my first boyfriend dumped me; he said I was unavailable. After that, I was the kid who went to school in the morning, went straight home after school, drank tea with my mother, and spent the rest of the day at home, catching up on cartoons.

The following year, I changed schools. I went to a high school outside my village. There was a rise in violence in the school that I was attending, and my sister and mother decided to move me to a safer school where they did not have to worry about my safety.

I was not in love with my first boyfriend; we would kiss. I never got used to kissing, even though he was not the first boy I kissed; it felt awkward. So, the break-up was a relief; I did not have to show up anymore. I dated him because he was kind and what the girls would call cute. My friend at the time also had a hand in me agreeing to date the guy; she had started dating already. She was tired of my singleness and wanted me to contribute to conversations instead of just listening all the time while she complained or praised her numerous boyfriends.

It was not easy to make new friends in the new school, as some of my friends were moved to different schools, and others remained in my old school. What made other learners converse with me was that I tried to stay academically up to speed; the goal was always to change the socioeconomic status at home. Within a few months in the new school, another kind boy asked me out; I accepted the proposal, primarily because of his manners; he was something I had never met before; he was so young and incredibly involved in church activities, and he was a pastor's son. We would talk about the bible a lot; if there were any religious activities in the school, he would take the lead.

I grew up in a Christian home, attended Sunday school for a couple of years, and attended church with my mother sometimes. After church, I was pretty done with the church for the week. Church once a week to keep the devil away, and the only other time I would read the bible at home was when my mother would ask me to read her something; either than that, the bible was a book to be seen at church; I was not religious or spiritual at all at that age. Surprisingly, he dumped me after a couple of months in the relationship, and when I asked him why, he also said I ignored him, and somehow, I was absent from the relationship. Well, I accepted and moved on with my life.

It was becoming a trend for me to get dumped for lack of attention or absenteeism in the relationship; it did not bother me much, but I needed to change my strategy. So, this time, I went off to the next boyfriend to go for outgoing guys who were not so quiet and timid anymore. An outgoing guy asked me out, and I accepted. Things were fantastic; we would spend time together during study time, but I still had the problem of going out during weekends; we dated during the week, I was never available on weekends, and I would stay home with my family.

Even that affair didn't go on for very long; just out of the blue, he did dump me. I say out of the blue because I never tend to see the break-ups coming. We are fine today, and the next thing, it's over; then I started thinking that maybe, just maybe, I was the problem. He broke up with me because I spent more time chatting and laughing with my guy friends, and he did not get attention when he was with me. I did not object to his decision; I accepted and moved on with life.

3| My Coming out Story

I took some time off from the dating scene to introspect a little. Something was happening inside me that made me absent from my early relationships. Let us back up a little to 1998. I am ten years old, freshly in grade five, and in a new school. I walk into my new class, and there are old faces I knew from the previous school and new ones I did not know. But, as I walked in, there was one new face to which I was glued. She was the most beautiful girl I had ever seen; she instantly became my reason for breathing.

It was love at first sight; from that day onward, I wanted to spend every moment with her. She felt the same, and she did not know it, but our spirits connected. She became my best friend; I saw her some weekends. She was my first love, my everything. She ruined any other relationship after her; I used her as a reference. I was her Valentine for two years; she grew older and broke my heart. She started taking an interest in boys, and I could not stand it; I had just to heal my broken heart. Even today, she has no idea how badly she broke my heart. I never felt the need to let her know. My first love, my crush.

I have always known that my attraction was more to females than males. I grew up playing with boys, from my neighbours to my cousins, and even in school, I was closer to boys than girls. The attraction to girls was always more intense and confused the hell out of my little fragile mind.

We had no TV or electricity at home until we returned to my grandparents' house. I had no information on sexual orientation from the media, and no one even spoke of my anomaly in my village. I was terrified. I tried to figure things out as I went through life.

Even when I had my first boyfriend, I was intrigued not by him but by my female classmates, and they always grabbed my attention more than all my boyfriends could. The most bizarre thing happened when I arrived at my new high school. I found these two girls fascinating; they were soccer players, out of the closet as lesbians. I had a strong interest in getting to know them and had all sorts of questions for them.

I had an innocent face, and when one of them greeted me, I jumped into the opportunity, and I was like, yes, this is it, I can finally get some answers; nothing could have prepared me for what happened next. Dzuni (not her real name) was kind enough to answer any question. I started spending more time with her; when I asked her what had happened to her and what made her this way, She said this is just how I am. I like girls the way a boy likes a girl, and I was like, and you are okay with that? She said she is okay with it because she cannot change it even if she wants to.

Other learners started noticing that I was spending all my free time with Dzuni, and they started gossiping and chit-chatting about our friendship behind our backs. Let me go a little deeper: our school offered boarding houses, and because she was from out of town, she stayed in the boarding houses, and I would stay in her room during break time. One day, she leaned over to kiss me during our afternoon talks; I could not resist. I responded positively, if you know what I mean; it felt so good; I had finally found the thing that had been missing from kissing my boyfriends: a girl.

Then we started spending even more time together; we became closer and closer by the day, and the noise around us became louder and louder. I was ashamed of our relationship. Everyone was staring at us all the time. Always pointing fingers at us, always saying how wrong it was, and those inclined to the Christian faith had more to say than the non-religious souls. I started second-guessing my feelings, questioning my whole existence; I was always in the background unless it was during lesson time. I have always had poor social skills and wanted people out of business, as I was never in anybody else's business. Finally, I cracked under all the attention; I went to Dzuni and told her it would be better if we did not see each other anymore. Dzuni was hurt by my sudden decision but accepted it.

Ha-Mphego is a small village, and we all knew each other's business; I was afraid that the talks in school would make it to my village, and I was not ready to deal with that.

I reintegrated back into the heterosexual (normal) club, and I figured the best way to do that was by dating a boy; nothing says heterosexual than a boy and a girl dating, right? I have never been so wrong in my life. Accepting to be with my third boyfriend was to prove my sexual orientation. It did not work. I was with him physically (not in a sexual manner), but he never had my mind and spirit.

I was drowning; the attraction toward girls was super intense, and I did not know what to do. By then, I was sixteen years old, and all my friends were having sex and talking about sex all the time; here, I thought that maybe if I did have sex, the feelings would go away, and I could be normal and happy. During my final year of high school, I would show up and do all I had to do, but I was an outcast on the inside before being an outcast outside of me.

I had gotten so good at hiding who I was that the pain felt normal; I figured that was my punishment for being the way I was. I did not deserve any better. So, I decided to become sexually active; if there is a chance that after doing it, I could be normal, I need to take that chance. All I remember about the day was a Saturday afternoon at the guy's place; he had no idea I was there to be cleansed. Then it happened; my innocence was gone forever, never to be seen again. All I wanted was for it to be over so I could usually show up the following Monday at school. But, man, it did not work. On Monday, I mean the Monday after I had lost my virginity, I was still lesbian. My world was shattered; I was more depressed now than I was as a virgin.

I finished high school, packed my bags, and attended university the following year. The fourth boyfriend has no idea what happened to me; I just disappeared. He called until he could not call anymore, and that was the end of our relationship. I hope he is okay.

4| Freedom Is Here

Getting accepted into university was easy; the hard part was producing registration fees. I will always be a proud supporter of the Fees Must Fall movement. My sister had to take out a loan for me to be able to register, and I will be forever grateful to her for that. I eventually got my financial aid within five months of registration, but I had to pay it back when I started working, and it took me two years to pay it off. For the rest of my three years, I received a fully funded bursary; the only thing I had to do to pay them back was to go work in Limpopo province after completion, which I did, and I am still working in Limpopo. My home province.

Back to relationships, I quickly fell in love in my first year of university. She was kind, funny, and very in tune with who she was, a heterosexual girl from Kwa Ndebele. We shared a student house on our arrival at the university. We became close friends until I started longing for more than just her friendship, but out of fear of rejection, I kept the feelings to myself for a few a month and only towards the end of the year I did manage to build myself up to confess my true feelings for her.

She was shocked by my confession and rejected me gently; we remained friends, but not for long. I believe that my confession of my love for her left a seed of curiosity in her mind, and it was reduplicating daily; long story short, she became my girlfriend. We were together for the remainder of the year and most of the following year. While I was with her, I slowly came to terms with my sexual orientation. Meeting more people who identified as LGBTQ somehow did put me at ease. The relationship was experimental for both of us; she was my first, and I was hers.

She was what I considered perfect. On the other hand, I was becoming a version of myself I had never met before; I was like a bird released into the wild for the first time and could fly freely. Now, I did not have to answer to anyone, and I just wanted to fly. I started experimenting with alcohol; one drink always led to ten more drinks and long nights of partying. I was out and drinking every weekend sometimes. Weekends I started on Thursdays.

I drank until I could not stand anymore on most days; drinking became a regular activity because it picked up my confidence; I could speak more freely to anyone; at this point, that innocent little girl was disappearing more every day. My drinking negatively affected my relationship; I would leave to see a friend at midday and would come back after midnight, hardly standing straight; she did open the door for me until she could not anymore. If she did not open it, I would find the closest party and continue with my drinking.

During all this, I found absolutely nothing wrong with my behaviour. I continued drinking and partying throughout my university, which was four years. However, I also figured out something else about myself: my sexual energy was intensifying from my second year. I wanted more and more; it seemed as if the more I engaged in sexual acts, the stronger it got, but that was not the worst part; the worst of it all was that I was having extra relationship affairs. I would sleep around, and it felt as if I could not control that energy at the time. Eventually, she ended that relationship, and I remained single and mingled until I completed my degree.

One-night stands and friends with benefits became my thing; I could easily be with two women on the same day. Do not get me wrong, I am not praising my behaviour; I am stating this to show the extent of my disease at the time. I did not know that my behaviour was a symptom of my trauma. I strongly believe in the saying that the first step to recovery is admitting a problem. This statement cuts across every situation that we may encounter in this life.

I did manage to complete the degree in record time because I still wanted to make my family proud in the middle of all the craziness. So, I made sure that I focused on my studies from Monday to Thursday if I did not have any tests or exams. My university life was separate from my life when I went home; it seemed like I had always lived a double life. My family was not aware of my sexual orientation for years, and in university, everyone knew my sexual orientation and my wild side. At home, I was still timid, shy, and innocent.

I came out of the closet to my family when I was in university. My sister did not stay far from where I was studying; I did visit her more often, and we reconnected in those years. One day, I did build enough courage to have that conversation with her. I just came out straight and said it because all the rehearsal conversations I had been playing in my head were driving me crazy, so I was like, sis, I am lesbian, and she was rather shocked; I mean, who would be, I'd never had a conversation like that or spoke of my love life with her until that moment. And then she asked me, what happened? Have boyfriends hurt you? What happened?

In my response, I told her nothing had happened; no one had hurt me. I had known that I was like this for many years. I had been scared to tell anyone because I did not want to be rejected by you or anyone. The fear of the unknown was my biggest enemy. My sister never left me; she continued to love and support me. Our relationship continued to blossom. I was extremely fortunate to have been born into this family.

I have friends whose coming-out stories did not have a happy conclusion; some became homeless, others were cut off financially, and others were disowned and rejected by their families. When God created heaven and earth, he deemed us all good and perfect as humans. We were created with the same perfection; how do we consider his creation imperfect and discard it as if the creator had made a mistake? Somehow, he had developed a model that needed to be fixed. That is a topic for another book. Parents, you do not have to have all the answers; take the creation back to the creator and ask Him, how do I navigate as a parent with this perfect being that you have entrusted me with? Go for therapy if you must; do not discard His ideal creation. My coming out did not happen all at once; I started with my sisters and waited to break the news to my parents later.

After the love affairs at university, I took a little break from the dating scene. I went home for the summer break before beginning my community service the following year, and I spent as much time at home helping my mother as possible. One afternoon, I decided to grab a drink in town, and just as I was enjoying a cold beer, I saw the most beautiful girl in the room. I smiled at her, and she smiled back at me. Within a few minutes, she had disappeared, and I sat there hoping she would return. She did not; later, I found out that she walked outside the club with a drink in her hand and was arrested for public drinking; what a way to start a relationship, LOL.

Anyway, when I got home that day, I could not stop thinking about her, so I thought, let me return to that club; I would see her again. Unfortunately, I could not return the following day as I had promised to help my mother at home. So, the day after, I went back to grab a drink and hopefully see the love of my life, and by the grace of the Gods, she was there; I didn't waste time not reaching out to her, only to find out that came back to the club yesterday hoping to see me, that is just some fairy tale stuff.

The connection was instant; we spent the rest of the afternoon chatting, drinking, and dancing. Finally, when it was time to go our separate ways, I couldn't let her go, so I did what any mature 21-year-old would do: I called my mother to let her know I would be back in the morning. I had just met a girl, and I was going to meet her parents at her place tonight; that was one of the craziest moments of my life, and my mother had no choice but to just go with it. So, we spent the rest of the night chatting; we spoke until we fell asleep, and we did not do it.

That was the beginning of my new relationship after university, technically my second girlfriend. I was a bit more mature, taking responsibility for my actions. I had parties and drank, but I was not like a fish anymore. I did not have any affairs outside my relationship. We were together for a year. It was beautiful; we were in love and spent most of the time together.

We saw each other every weekend, and I even met her family during the day. They knew we were together and were civil about it, but they did not accept the relationship. They did not accept the relationship, and it ended when they gave her an ultimatum, saying she had to choose between them and me. Unfortunately, she chose them. I did not hold the decision against her, but it hurt like hell. It took me forever to get over the fact that we were over.

I fell back into my comfort zone, parties, alcohol, and girls. I was drunk from Thursday to Sunday again; I showed up for work but never gave my best. I was shattered; I thought I had found my one true love, and man was I wrong. In the time that I spent with her, I learned the value of authenticity; even though her parents ended up folding to the pressure of society, she never once hid who she was from them, even when they wanted her to end things with me, they knew that being with me was a true reflection of who she was, I salute her for that. Even though she got to meet my parent, she was my friend to them; they only knew the truth after we had broken up.

5| Girl Marries Girl

As a young girl, I never daydreamed about my future wedding day. The concept of getting married simply didn't occur to me. As I grew older, societal expectations led to frequent inquiries about my marital status. In response, I consistently stated that I would get married at 30. Surprisingly, this prediction came true: I got married at 30. It's a reminder to be mindful of our words, as the universe has a way of bringing them to fruition.

I met my ex-wife at my workplace not long after my break-up. At that time, I wasn't actively seeking a new relationship; I was content with how things were in my life and devoted to caring for my mother and sisters. She was new in town, and I lived there for about a year. What drew me to her was not just her kindness and friendliness but also her captivating innocence, which piqued my curiosity. It wasn't a sexual interest at first; rather, I was intrigued by her as a person and wanted to explore a deeper connection with her.

She was a Muslim Indian woman surrounded by African Christians; I wanted to know her. We became good friends; we would sit together in meetings since she did not know many people, hang out after work, she would cook dinner, and invite me to eat with her. I could not get enough of her cooking; the food was spicy at first, but I got used to the heat of the spices as the weeks went by. Finally, I got so accustomed to the spices that I started eating spicier food than her. During our relationship, when I did cook, she would complain that the food was too spicy, and for me, that was the right amount of heat.

The more time we spent together, the more I enjoyed spending time with her. However, because of what I had gone through in my previous relationship, I never stopped seeing other people, even though I fell in love with her. At the time, I did not realise the extent of my brokenness and what it was doing to me every day, so it was business.

It is early 2011, and I visited my sister during the Easter holidays. As usual, I had a little too much to drink, so I picked up the phone and called and confessed my dying love for her, which I regretted in the morning. I asked her to please forget about the conversation. She did not; she brought it up when I came back home. I continually said, "Please let it go." I did not know that such an idea had crossed her mind before.

A few weeks passed, and we continued our usual conversations while sharing meals. One weekend, I was going about my weekend business. I was drinking and having a good time, and she texted to say, if we are going to do this, we must do it right. I was drunk, so without even thinking much about it, I was like I am in. After sobering up, I just remembered, and the questions flooded my thoughts: what did I have just signed up for? I had to think about the conversation. (do not make decisions when you are drunk) Primarily, she is Muslim; our values and principles are worlds apart, mainly because I am making up my values as I go.

I finally came to my senses and said let me commit to this relationship and see how things unfold. I wanted to take things slow and get to know each other. She did not want that. We spent lots of time together. If we were apart, we would be on the phone the whole time. I started to feel as if the walls around me were caving in, and I couldn't breathe; I was used to doing what I wanted, and when I wanted, I craved space and was too scared to talk about it with her for months, and I would just go with the flow. Those were some of the signals that the universe was sending me, that you need to heal woman, slow down, and did l listen? Hell no. So, I went on autopilot and kept afloat.

When I first encountered my ex-wife, she exuded an air of fragility and vulnerability. My entrance into her life seemed to bring a glimmer of hope to her eyes. Hearing about the depth of her past traumas, I instinctively put her needs above my own, aiming to shield her from any further pain. Little did I realise that I wasn't equipped to handle the complexities of her situation, as I had grappled with my trauma in ways that were far from ideal. Despite her perception that I had everything under control, I eventually realised I did not.

Because she only saw her kids on weekends, she applied for a transfer to work closer to them. So, I stayed behind, and she would visit me with the kids on weekends. I knew she had kids, but I had never met them until they visited. The first weekend, I was extremely uncomfortable. I have not been a kid's person my whole life. Don't get me wrong, I cared for my baby sisters and nephews. It was fun and games because they had a place where they belonged; they did not belong with me. I have never seen myself playing the motherly role; it was an adjustment.

Things got even worse when I had to spend every weekend with them; I felt like an outsider who did not know how to get in and be part of what was inside. During the week, I spent time alone where I worked, and on weekends, I had to adjust to the unfamiliar environment. I booked a few therapy sessions to navigate this new journey; the therapist suggested a few tools I could use to make the adjustment easy and smoother. After a few sessions and practice, I started to feel like an insider, not fully inside, but it was better than being outside.

As I struggled to adjust, I never took the time to think about what it would have been like for them. They were young, but I am sure they were in turmoil with themselves as much as I was; sometimes, your wounds will consume you so much that you do not even stop to recognise how others are being affected by the same situation that you are in with them.

When I broke ties with all the other girls to focus on this new relationship, I thought I had conquered that side of me. And I was wrong yet again. When I spent my time alone during the week, I entertained other girls. Then, after work, I would fool around and flirt with them, not forgetting the drinks. My ex-wife had never sipped an alcoholic beverage until she met me. She experimented with a few but could not stand the smell or taste.

The fooling around continued for almost two years; I had gotten so good at living a double life that it came naturally. I would spend the whole week with a girl, and she did not exist on the weekends, so I was not with her until I saw her again. This behaviour only fed my ego; it grew more prominent each time I behaved that way. Things have gotten so bad that I only thought I could break the chain if I moved in with her and the kids; indeed, I would behave better if we stayed together.

I came to the realisation that despite my physical relocation, my internal struggles and behaviours remained unchanged. I found myself grappling with the same thoughts and trauma, leading to a lack of transformation in my actions. Even as I adhered to my usual work routine, I sought validation during lunchtime to feed my ego. Additionally, I found it challenging to resist succumbing to sexual attraction, often attributing it to mere chemistry in most instances.

Chemistry is when you meet someone, and both of you feel something is happening, but you do not know what it is. I learned later in life that you can have chemistry with many people and not base your actions on chemistry alone; you need more than that. So, a word of advice: please do not be a slave to your chemistry. It feels good, but you will have to feel good with many people, and after that, you are empty. I was a true slave to chemistry, and what made things worse was that when I would get home, I would drink from the chemistry I had experienced during the day to keep my girlfriend happy.

I used the rush from my chemistry partner to fuel my chemistry at home. Whenever the outside chemistry was taken away, I would be reactive to her chemistry only because I was so occupied with feeding my ego that I missed the prominent part that I had to play in cultivating our chemistry and connectedness as a couple. She was left cultivating by herself, and we could not reap the same if I had not worked.

I used to be very disconnected from myself and my partner, both emotionally and mentally. It's painful that I failed to comprehend her perspective whenever my partner tried to address our problems. It felt like she spoke in a language I couldn't understand. I often brushed off our conversations, leaving her feeling unheard and frustrated. Over time, it became a repetitive cycle, and I grew weary of hearing the same concerns. I occasionally promised to make improvements but could not follow through due to a lack of understanding and awareness.

I was oblivious to my reality. From my perspective, I was working hard for the relationship; I was always there when she needed me, I gave her what she wanted when she wanted it, and I realised later that I had become my father. You provide the materials your family needs and leave the emotional things out. My father ensured we had food, clothes, and shelter, which is how he showed his love, and I did the same. I came to that realisation along the way; that is just how he showed his love to us; it is the only way he knew how. I had the power to present my passion sufficiently; if I did not like how my father displayed his love, why was I doing the same thing with which I was not happy? I had to work on it; I am still a work in progress.

She always said that I seemed happier whenever I was with other people than when I was with her. I would let my hair down, laugh with other people, and have an enjoyable time, but when it came to her and me, a wall blocked her from accessing me. I was right in front of her, yet so far away from her; I was not warm to be around or cold.

Along the way, things got so bad that I was always busy; I had a hectic schedule on which I did not compromise. The only thing it did was build a thicker bridge between her and me; the harder she tried to reach me, the further away from her I would go. My daily schedule looked something like this:

3h30: Wake up for pre-workout.

4h00: Gym time

5h00: Get ready for work.

6h00: Leave for work.

I am already up for two and a half hours, and she is not a part of it. It gets worse.

18h00: Back from work

18h30: Gym time

19h30: Bath and dinner time

We stayed together for ten years, and I am sure she can count the number of days we had dinner together; we had dinner together when we were friends more than when we were dating. I kept so busy even on weekends; I would do all the house chores and be so tired by the end of the day that she was left alone, and I did not recognise my crimes. She was alone in the relationship, and I found no excuse in the book to make it look as if she was wrong.

As I have mentioned, she was wounded as well, and at some point, I had mastered using that to my advantage; I would make her doubt her truth because mine made more sense; she would be viewing things from a place of fear rather than her true self. She had been abandoned, hurt, and disappointed so many times that she feared being alone. I mistreated her, and she knew that even though I was not aware of my actions at the time, she would justify my behaviour so we would be together. The one constant thing was that I never left; I was always there, even if it was not how she wanted me. I was there.

I have only realised my emotionally abusive nature as I am writing this confession. I have emotionally abused her for years. I have manipulated her so many times that it became natural for me. I did the manipulation to get away with what I was doing behind her back. Being with me meant she had to part ways with her immediate family, parents, and siblings. They all wanted nothing to do with her; she had to choose between them and me and decided to be with me. So she could be herself instead of being judged by them.

Being with me meant they cast the judgment for the last time; she knew who was in her corner and who was not. I was always by her corner, supported her dreams and ambitions, and validated her in times of doubt. And she craved that as it was something she had never received from her family. As soon as her immediate family knew about us, they spread the message, and even cousins and aunties disowned her.

There were times that I wanted to leave her because I knew that she deserved better. Still, each time, I would mention that she would fall apart and have deep depression, anxiety, and other things related to deep emotional stress. I have made her alienate her family, and now I am all she has, so I must stay. I can continue doing what I am doing; as long as I stay with her, we will be okay; that is what I use as justification each time.

I met her when I was 23 years old, and 7 years later, we are getting married. She always wanted to get married; it is part of her religious values and principles. As for me, I was thirty now, and I thought it was the universe telling me it was time I got married. This is the step that will change things for me. We were not in a good space when we spoke about getting married. Deep down, I knew I should not do it, but there was another part, the part that could not leave her; that said, things will get better after you get married.

After agreeing to get married, I stopped all my affairs and broke off all communication that may have been there. I was ready for a fresh start to married life. I have heard people say that things get better after getting married. I have never worked on my relationship in all the years, and this magic event changes a relationship in the blink of an eye. I thought this was my chance to make things better for her.

My mother and sisters were part of the wedding. We flew them to Cape Town and made a holiday out of it. My younger sisters had not been to Cape Town, so it was an excellent experience for them that will permanently be attached to my wedding day. When I introduced her to my family, they were shocked and concerned. Firstly, it was the 10 years of age gap; secondly, her ethnicity; and thirdly, she already had children.

The introduction happened incredibly early in our relationship, as it was essential to her that she be known as my girlfriend; again, it was about values for her. I tried to convince her of my readiness or unreadiness for family introductions. She felt rejected and did not want to listen to me. I folded, and she introduced her to my mother.

There was always a disconnect between her and my mother, primarily due to the language barrier; my mother barely speaks English, and she cannot speak Tshivenda. Secondly, the values, in the village things are done differently in town, and if you spend more time inside the house, you would be labelled as lazy, because the work is outside the house, and you are spending time inside. She felt as if I was always busy and taking care of her. My mother eventually understood the dynamics of our relationship, and she accepted the relationship. One day, she said something very profound. She said Rendani, I prayed to God for a child, and I did not specify the sexual orientation, and therefore, I am happy that God answered my prayers. Due to that, she accepted me without judgment; it does not mean she was not concerned, she was, but sometimes you must let people learn from their own mistakes.

I went back and forth before agreeing to get married. We had decided to take a break not long before the wedding. During that time, I was trying very hard to figure out why I was the way I was; I made an appointment to go see a therapist, and after a long session of talking, the only thing that was left for me to do was to pack my bags and go work on myself, the environment I was in was not conducive for the work that I had to do, that what the therapist made me realise. I had to isolate myself and examine myself inwardly. I did not do that; I did the opposite; I stayed. Therapy only works if you are willing to put in the work; I realised that only after I had not done the work and found myself in the same situation repeatedly.

Here I was, 30 years old, in the beautiful city of Cape Town, with my family and my lovely bride with her daughter. I was leaving my life behind and entering a new life as a married and renewed woman. Leaving behind also meant losing some friends. There are friends that I did not even tell I was getting married, and they did not even support me getting married because they knew I was not being authentic about it. And at that time, we went our separate ways.

The wedding was intimate, with very few people. She looked like the perfect bride. We had a short ceremony led by an Islamic maulana. We exchanged our vows and signed the papers. I felt transformed. I believed every word I said. I did not realise that the words came from the cracks of my wounds, and what was about to disentangle was something I never expected.

In the first year of marriage, I actively ensured I was present. I stayed home more, did not entertain any thoughts of affairs, and avoided anything that might trigger the unmarried version of me. Most days, I would be miserable and not interested in anything. Our intimacy faded with the wind. I would use the guilt from being with other women as motivation to be with her intimately, but now my well was dry; I had nowhere to drink from. That crushed her even more, and no matter how hard I tried, it was just not working. It had gotten to a point where she stopped trying because she would get rejected.

After a year of marriage, I returned to my old ways. I met someone I had known for a few years, but we were not close. I did not even think about her much until an incident left us instantly connected. We both agreed that we could not pursue that connection further and had to cut the cord as quickly as possible. We did that for at least a couple of weeks. However, we continued getting to know each other, and the more we spent time together, the stronger the bond became.

We had so much in common and would spend hours together; the fact that what we were doing was wrong never seemed to leave our minds, but even that did not stop us from spending even more time together. After a few months, we realised we had fallen in love with each other, and we kept going. Before we knew it, we talked about our future together. This relationship so consumed me; it gave my life some excitement, something to look forward to. We continued with the affair for two years. We did our best to keep it a secret; anyone who would ask me about the affair, I would say no, especially those whom my wife knew. I understood that one day, the secret would come out in the open, and I did not want them implicated in my web of lies.

In my mind, I was protecting them by not telling them. They felt betrayed when I came clean to them, but I did what I felt was best. My ex-wife only found out about the affair after my marriage and the romance had ended. I went on for years keeping this big secret, and the one who got to tell my ex-wife was the person who was part of the affair. She asked me a couple of times to come clean to my ex-wife about the affair, and I said to her, it's of no use; she is dealing with the end of the marriage, and you want to add something that was in the past into the mix of her trauma, then I said to her if it would give her peace, she should tell her herself.

Indeed, one evening I received a call from my ex-wife, asking me how I did such a thing, and I was like crap; she came clean. I kept calm, allowing her to speak her mind, and all I could say was that I was sorry for everything that had transpired. There was nothing else that I could say that would make things any better for her. I have always wondered if she would have come clean if she and I were still together, but that was not the critical aspect in this situation; I must reflect and remove everyone from the equation and only leave me; what can Rendani do from this point forward?

In this journey called life, I have learned that if you look outside of yourself for answers, which is when the pity party begins. It comes with many other destructive ideas; looking in the mirror in challenging situations is hard, but the only way out is through. Blaming others for doing what they did will not solve anything. All I do is reflect and change my behaviour, and I can quickly control how I move forward.

When I ended the marriage, it was the scariest thing I have ever done; I would rehearse the speech for days and still say nothing to her; it took everything inside of me to mention to her that I had reached the endpoint in this relationship, I can't do this anymore; obviously, she didn't just say okay, and that was it, she came up with all the scenarios that were supposed to keep us together, I was tired, and I couldn't say yes anymore. So, I said no that day, and I meant it.

After some months, she could see that there was no turning back for me, and therefore, she accepted my decision; it was tough for her to come to terms with the decision. I did my best to be sensitive to the whole situation. We stayed together for a year after ending the marriage; we had to finalise the coordination of our separation and make it as smooth as possible. I hope our paths will meet again from a place of healing and not of pain one day.

6| Going Back to the Creator

One of the main reasons I had to end the relationship was the realisation that I was not living; I had reduced myself to being part of the population count in South Africa; I was not an expression of who the creator had created me. I found refuge in my journey of spiritual awakening. I had never been a religious or spiritual person before, but I had a spiritual awakening that shook my world upside down in the last two years. I am still a student of my spirituality, and through the journey of getting to know myself, I had to take a U-turn. I had to return to where I came from and let go of what I had learned to reclaim my identity.

I had to experience the true meaning of being born again. Not being born again religiously, as I had done before, it was nothing like that. I had to walk back into my mother's womb to experience my rebirth. Reclaiming who you are is the most challenging thing to do, but nature does not always take the straightforward way out but the necessary route to get the desired results.

Most days, I wanted to quit and return to what is familiar to me because now I am walking in the wilderness by myself and putting my faith in those who have walked this earth before me. However, in the journey, I realised that most of the cuts I had were deeper wounds; when I spent time dealing with them one by one, not dressing them up with pretty plaster but digging and reaching deeper into each one of them, that was necessary for me to get to the roots of my dis-ease and find natural healing.

All the healing that I had to go through was a spiritual awakening; it was not me who said I was ready to change; the universe adjusted and realigned me to my destiny. My destiny could not be reached in my false being state; it would be through my most authentic form. The relationships outside of me changed automatically when I began to work on my relationship with myself. I had never taken the time to deal with my mind, body, and spirit holistically. They were constantly divided. The three spheres of my being had to be merged to serve me as one whole being.

I have always been terrified of change. I wanted things to stay the same most of my life, but during my healing process, I recognised that change was the only way out for me. So, I had to part ways with many people in my life, the kind of conversations I used to have and the things that used to interest me; all those things have changed, and I became a stranger to myself. And the best part of this journey is that I have never been happier in my life.

It is still early to say that I have dealt with all my wounds because the journey continues for as long as I live. There is always room to learn more and to improve. Healing always occurs in stages, and I do not know what is next, but I know I will gladly accept and embrace the set.
This writing was part of my healing journey.

Thank you!

9 788119 524471

Printed at Repro India Ltd.